Older people and homelessness

A story of greed, violence, conflict and ruin

Derek Hawes

The POLICY PRESS

First published in Great Britain in 1997 by

The Policy Press
University of Bristol
Rodney Lodge
Grange Road
Bristol BS8 4EA

Telephone: (0117) 973 8797
Fax: (0117) 973 7308
E-mail: tpp@bris.ac.uk
Website: http://www.bris.ac.uk/Publications/TPP

©   The Policy Press, 1997

ISBN 1 86134 067 2

Photograph © Dewi Lewis, London.

Derek Hawes is lecturer in housing policy at the School for Policy Studies, University of Bristol.

Cover design by Qube Design Associates, Bristol.
Printed in Great Britain by Arrowhead Books Limited, Reading.

Preface

This publication derives from a research project undertaken with the assistance of an Economic and Social Research Council (ESRC) grant and sets out to establish the rates of growth in homelessness among older people and to analyse both the causes and the responses of the local authorities who carry the duty to offer accommodation under the 1985 Housing Act.[*]

Care has been taken to inform the results with an understanding of the perceptions of older people who are, or were themselves homeless.

The phenomenon of older homelessness is a difficult one to research for a number of practical and technical reasons referred to in Chapter 2. Characterised by an earlier writer (Crane, 1994) as "elusive and slippery" – an epithet for both the concepts and the subjects of enquiry – the task is made more problematic by the lack of agreement about who should be encompassed in the term 'older' and by the growing number of vagrant or 'street' homeless who rarely fall within the statutory local authority procedures for dealing with those who are both homeless and 'vulnerable due to old age'.

Therefore, the statistics utilised from official sources present only a partial picture of the scale of homelessness among elderly people. It has been essential to broaden the investigation to embrace the wider phenomenon and to accept that the original intention to confine the research to 'pensioner homelessness' has had to be abandoned in favour of a more realistic approach. In short, it has been necessary to incorporate those who fall through the welfare net or who, because of physical or psychological problems or through discharge from prison or other institutions, find themselves homeless in later life.

For these people, many of whom are between 50 and 60, the simple lack of accommodation is part of a far more intricate pattern of deprivation; they are what one researcher has termed the "chronically homeless" (Crane, 1994).

---

[*] During the course of this project new regulations and a new Code of Guidance consequent upon the 1996 Housing Act were presaged which are likely to have important implications for the way in which councils deal with homeless people. The issues arising for older homeless applicants are dealt with in the next chapter.

Contents

List of tables

1
Introduction

There are two distinct kinds of response to those who find themselves without a settled home in later life. First, there are those who are assessed and assisted by local authority housing departments under the duties imposed by the 1985 Housing Act and the more recent 1996 Act with the Code of Guidance relating thereto.

Second, the less formal, haphazard and varied responses made to those older people who do not approach local authorities and who, in addition to having no settled home, may be coping with physical or psychological difficulties, recent discharge from an institution, or lack of any family, financial or social resources. Many of the latter category may be abandoned to the streets and may well be dependant upon drugs or alcohol. Crane (1994) refers to these people as "chronically homeless", a term which will be utilised in this study.

By the summer of 1995 many local authority housing practitioners were reporting informally a growth in the numbers of people presenting as homeless who were being accepted for rehousing due to vulnerability as a result of old age. Much of this anecdotal comment seemed at odds with the claims by government departments that statutory homelessness was falling consistently after 1992. At the same time, concerns were being expressed by many in the housing and care fields that despite the introduction of community care policies and the recognition that housing was an important ingredient in effective care in the community, many older people were, in some sense, falling through the net of provision (Arblaster et al, 1996).

The approach of this research has therefore been to examine, for the period 1992 to 1995, just how far the official statistics support the anecdotal and impressionistic perceptions of practitioners and project workers to establish whether there is a significant growth in older homelessness and if so, the scale and spatial distribution of it. Secondly, the approach of this research has been to investigate the causes of loss of accommodation among older people and thirdly, the kinds of responses made by local authorities who accept these applicants as priority cases for rehousing.

A fourth purpose has been to consider to what extent there is scope for a convergence of policy – is there a possibility that strategies for dealing with older homelessness can be assisted by strategies for dealing with increasing void properties, particularly in areas where councils are facing either an excess of sheltered housing or a substantial problem of difficult-to-let sheltered accommodation?

It is necessary, however, to acknowledge that the numbers presenting to the homeless sections of local authority housing departments as both homeless and vulnerable due to old age do not afford a comprehensive or quantitatively accurate picture of the problem. The research objectives have thus been extended to estimate the scale of homelessness among those older people who, for various reasons, do not form part of the official statistics.

Such people may use hostels, night shelters or other informal networks of vagrancy or have been accommodated from the streets by informal or voluntary projects designed for the purpose.

The 1996 Housing Act

New regulations and guidance issued under Parts VI and VII of the 1996 Housing Act, and in particular *Statutory instrument 1996 No: 2754 The homeless*, will significantly alter the local authority response to older homeless people. They took effect on 20 January 1997. Further regulations covering detailed aspects of waiting lists and allocations were published some months later.

Part VII modifies the duties owed by a local authority towards homeless people. Someone who is statutorily homeless and in priority need will be rehoused for a period of up to two years (renewable) and cannot be offered security of tenure. The authority does not have to rehouse them if there is alternative accommodation available, for example, in the private sector.

The Act uses the framework of the 1985 Act as a starting point for redefining authorities' duties to homeless people. The most important changes are a new duty to provide advice and information about homelessness and its prevention; a closer definition of intentional homelessness with emphasis on collusion and on failure to take advice or assistance offered.

Duties towards asylum seekers and refugees are defined more closely and Section 193 contains a new provision that an authority's duty will be for up to two years. An authority has no duty, under Section 197 if it is satisfied that alternative accommodation is available locally.

The guidance issued makes clear that permanent housing can be offered only to people on a housing register which authorities must establish under Section 162 of the Act, but that there should be ample scope within an allocation scheme to allow for discretion to meet a person's care and support needs. New procedures are promised to ensure that assessment and referral by another agency can be dealt with within the allocation rules. However, there are indications from the new Labour government installed in May 1997 that these provisions may, in due course, be relaxed, and that homelessness will regain the priority which it enjoyed in the 1985 Act.

2
Methodology

The research methods employed in this project have, of necessity, been multi-layered and are set out below. This is followed by a discussion of the particular problems which face those researching homelessness and old age.

Statistical sources

~ The main statistical material is derived from Department of the Environment (DoE) and Welsh Office databases; in particular, an analysis was undertaken of the composite returns from local authorities (DoE form P1(E)(Housing)), for 1992 to 1995, which indicates authorities' activities in the area of homelessness and trends over the four-year research period.

~ These overall figures have been refined via a postal questionnaire to a random, stratified sample of 50 local authority homeless departments, comprising 40 district councils, four London boroughs and six metropolitan boroughs. It sought more detailed breakdowns of figures relating specifically to older people, including definitions used, responses made, causes of applicants' loss of home and local policy frameworks established. There was a 70% response to this questionnaire.

Detailed case studies

From the results of the postal questionnaire two processes were devised to elicit greater understanding of the apparent growth in older homelessness and the way in which officers are dealing with it; also to explain local perceptions of the possibilities for policy convergence in the responses devised by local authorities. These were:

~ face-to-face interviews with a selection of homelessness officers from the authorities surveyed;

~ two 'focus group' discussions with county group meetings of homelessness officers in which anomalies in the data, differences of practice and variations in interpretation were exposed and debated.

Understanding the chronically homeless

~ Interviews and telephone discussions were held with three voluntary project leaders of schemes for the rehousing and resettlement of street homeless and others with long-term lack of secure and permanent accommodation. Also, the records of national charities such as 'Crisis' and Homeless Network were perused.

~ The research methodology and early findings were discussed at a meeting arranged by the Housing Associations Charitable Trust (HACT), of researchers, campaigners and practitioners from throughout the UK, working in this field.

Case histories

A series of mini case histories were compiled from informal discussions with older people who had been homeless, as a means of illuminating the routes into and the prime causes of homelessness and the experience of the 'system' through which rehousing or re-settlement occurred.

Comparative commentary

While the prime theatre for the project has been English local authorities, the outcomes have been enriched by reference to comparative statistics in Wales and Scotland and by brief analysis of earlier research in the UK and in the USA.

The methodological problems encountered

The research faced some difficulties both of data interpretation and of practice in the field. For example:

Old age: the most important of these is the lack of agreement as to what constitutes 'old age' in relation to responding to home-lessness. The 1985 Housing Act requires that those who are vulnerable due to old age are given priority, but does not specify a particular age; however, the Code of Guidance issued to authorities suggests that all applications from people over 60 should be considered carefully (para 6.10). In practice, local authorities operate a wide range of approaches.

Many of those dealing with the street homeless argue that living a vagrant life can cause earlier ageing and will consider anyone of 50 and over for assistance (Rich, Rich and Mullins, 1995)

Homelessness: some disagreement exists about what constitutes homelessness. The DoE Code of Guidance includes not only those without a roof at all, but people under threat of losing their home, those with homes who, for specific reasons such as threat of violence, cannot utilise them, and those whose homes are inadequate or unsuitable for other than temporary use or are too expensive.

Some of the people interviewed for earlier research, referred to in Chapter 3, have existed in night shelters, hostels and friends' homes for years and have chosen to consider these transitional locations as their permanent mode of living. We are therefore faced with differing perceptions – shades of homeless-ness which include a range of people whom Rossi (1989) defines as "precariously housed" and in which about the only common factor is an extreme manifestation of poverty and residential instability (Bassuck and Buckner, 1992).

3
Setting the context

Perhaps the first principle in the study of ageing and the problems associated with it is that of heterogeneity – there is no such phenomenon as *the aged* (Sheppard, 1995). The population of older people contains widely differing sub-groups and, indeed sub-age groups: just as clearly, the category of older homelessness is demonstrably made up of a number of groups and causes. Economists of ageing have found that income distribution of the 60+ population reveals one of the largest indexes of inequality in income distribution – a fact that the reliance on median scales of income can obscure, hiding the vast difference between the highest and lowest (Rich, Rich and Mullins, 1995).

It is also evident that in examining the causes and growth in older homelessness we must look beyond the immediate factors such as mental health problems or physical impairment, family dysfunction or alcohol abuse, to exogenous factors such as inadequate housing policy, benefits regimes and employment circumstances, over which the individual is often powerless to exert influence. As Crane (1994) emphasises, "that elderly people are homeless in contemporary Western society commands both sociological and welfare interest".

Earlier research reviewed

Although in the 1960s and 1970s studies of homeless men in London and the USA showed that between 27% and 35% found in shelters and temporary hostels, or on the streets, were over 60, little was suggested by way of cause or remedy; at that time a British study also found that 18% of those sleeping rough were 60+ (Lodge Patch, 1971). But more recent research and academic commentary on homelessness in the UK has paid

scant attention to the specific phenomenon of older people who lose their accommodation. Indeed, it is difficult to disagree with Crane's conclusion that our understanding of the issues is 'rudimentary', especially in regard to the relative importance of the personal and structural causes of this 'exceptional' behaviour (Crane, 1994).

A 1993 study of single homelessness for the DoE by York University included 225 'over 60s' interviewees among its sample of 1,763 people. 80% of these were in temporary shelter and 20% were sleeping rough. 16% said their loss of home was due to the death of a spouse or close friend and a further 7% blamed a relationship breakdown. Other main causes cited were eviction (7%), closure of a property (8%) and rent or mortgage arrears (6%) (Anderson et al, 1993). This study, however, had nothing to say about underlying influences or about the difference between those who were only recently rendered homeless and those who had a longer and more persistent experience of chronic homelessness. In 1993 Crane also studied street homelessness in inner London, targeting 50 of those aged 60 and over; her study provided an in-depth profile which discussed their motivations, "street history", behaviour, and health as well as their preferences in regard to accommodation (Crane, 1993).

Specific recommendations are made in Crane's work concerning the need for further research, for more services and specific interventions, drawing heavily upon responses made in cities in the USA.

More recent research completed in 1996 by the London Research Centre (LRC) found that nine out of ten councils reported increases in applications from vulnerable people, many of whom were elderly, who it was claimed, were homeless as a result of failures in the community care system. (See LRC, 1996.)

An earlier examination of the British experience in this field, by the Audit Commission, which concentrated on the local authority process for dealing with cases under the 1985 Housing Act, points out that despite the legislative duty on housing departments, many older people sleep on the streets each night (Audit Commission, 1989). However, the Audit Commission, despite making 35 recommendations, had no advice to offer on dealing with such elderly people.

Most recently, Crane has returned to her earlier work in order to re-examine more closely the causes and scale of chronic homelessness and to highlight some of the developing examples of good practice which have emerged in British cities (Crane, 1997).

This work confirms the paucity of good data, the significant incidence of mental illness and the multiplicity of causes underlying the lack of a safe home among those whom Crane terms 'lifetime' homeless, 'mid-life' homeless and 'late-life' homeless, she finds that "no policies and few homeless services are targeted specifically at older homeless people".

Experience from the USA

In the USA, where many more studies of older homelessness have been undertaken, recent work echoes the view of British researchers that there is ambiguity and lack of consensus both about what constitutes homelessness and what is defined as old age. All have included people who have access to marginal or temporary shelter, and 'flop-houses' (Douglass et al, 1988; Cohen and Sokolovsky, 1989; Rich, Rich and Mullins, 1995).

Most American work includes people in their 50s. Indeed Rich, Rich and Mullins, whose sample included 72.5% of people between 50 and 60, argue that the generally accepted age in the literature is 50+ and that over 50s may be considered old because stresses, nutritional problems and untreated health conditions contribute to premature ageing.

In the British context it might be difficult to apply this argument to those who present immediately after losing a secure home, to local authorities, although the case should certainly be made in regard to those with longer term accommodation, instability and vagrancy histories.

Douglass et al interviewed 68 men and 17 women aged 54+ in Detroit and noted such factors as lifelong difficulties in relating to other people as a major factor in homelessness, accompanied by a lack of family support, criminal behaviour and drug dependency. Discharge from an institutional context was the major immediate factor in lack of a home (Douglass et al, 1988).

In New York, Cohen and Sokolovsky were more concerned with understanding the coping mechanisms among chronic homeless men and the means they use to survive on 'Skid Row'. Their sample of over 280 were aged 50 and above, among whom they found psychological trauma as a result of breakdowns in relationships, alcohol abuse and inability to hold a job, all combining to induce people to 'choose' homelessness in what an earlier researcher has termed 'retreatist' behaviour (Merton, 1957).

Tampa Bay Florida is, for reasons of climate and geography, something of a mecca for retired people from all over the USA and is thus a good site in which to examine the relationship between age-concentrated populations and homeless older people. Rich, Rich and Mullins have researched older homelessness, sampling 103 inhabitants who use such services as soup kitchens, temporary shelters and clothing replacement stores.

They construct a profile of the characteristics and needs of the sample and the service and policy implications for the authorities, with particular recommendations in regard to housing policy and the pertinence of social service relief programmes. They advocate targeting those at risk of homelessness and supporting the poorest with preventive measures.

The stereotyping of both ageing and homelessness, and their distorting effects on US policy is examined in depth. Innovative interventions and empowerment strategies are discussed against a background in which the plight of younger families without a home has obscured a growth in the incidence of homelessness among the over-50s, similar in scale and cause to that of the British Isles (Rich, Rich and Mullins, 1995).

The pertinence of the US experience in this field is that considerably more research has been done there than in the UK and that the pattern of US housing policy, which relies heavily on market forces and private provision, presages the direction in which UK policy is heading. The concept of low-cost social housing assumes a largely private sector basis of supply with reducing levels of centrally provided benefits to the individual.

4
The research findings

The statistical profile

The numbers of homeless families in England accepted for rehousing by local authorities rose steadily throughout the 1980s and reached a peak in 1991 of 144,780, of whom 137,250 were found to be in priority need, as defined in the DoE's then Code of Guidance. These figures have fallen in each subsequent year although the peak quarter for acceptances was actually the March quarter of 1992, thus making the actual peak the year ending March 1992, when the annual total rose to 145,080.

In the period covered by this research (1992-95), the annual figures show a steady decline after the first quarter, with 1992 representing the highest year, followed by an annual percentage drop of between 3% and 7.5% (see Table 1). The cases in priority need drop from 138,700 to 116,940, a reduction of over 16%. Overall, by December 1995, as defined by the official statistics, homelessness had declined by 17% from a peak in March 1992.

Within these figures there were also a series of reductions, for example, in the numbers in Bed & Breakfast hotels, in short-life accommodation and other temporary homes, including women's refuges. Substantial percentage reductions in these categories occur each quarter during the four years under review.

However, in the same four-year period, the proportion of cases of those deemed to be vulnerable by reason of old age and accepted as in priority need only fell marginally by 4% and actually grew as a percentage of the whole, from 4.49% of the total (6,230) found to be in priority need in 1992 to 5.13% (5,950) in 1995 (see Table 1).

In all 50 of the authorities sampled through the postal survey, the numbers in this category increased in at least three of the four years under review. In many, the percentage increases were large, but given the very low starting point, the increase in numbers is less dramatic (see Appendix). For example, East Cambridgeshire had housed two cases by reason of old age in 1992 and this increased in each subsequent year to 11 in 1995. Trafford Metropolitan Borough Council dealt with 50 in 1992, growing to 77 in 1994 and reducing to 66 in 1995.

Other examples, set out in Table 2 and taken from differing kinds of authority, demonstrate the spatial similarity of the trend.

Table 1: People accepted as unintentionally homeless and in priority need by local authorities in England (1992-95)

	1992	1993	1994	1995
Total acceptances	142,890	132,380	122,460	120,810
Total in priority need	138,700	127,630	118,490	116,940
Total vulnerable through old age	6,230	5,920	6,050	5,950
Older cases as a % of whole	4.49	4.63	5.10	5.13

Source: DoE forms PI(E) (Housing) 1992-95

Table 2: Increases in cases of older homelessness by regional distribution of authority (1992-95)

Authority	1992	1993	1994	1995
Carrick	14	16	18	29
Peterborough	7	6	16	16
Plymouth	54	54	60	61
Tewkesbury	2	8	6	9
South Somerset	13	23	25	33
Crawley	10	15	17	18
Newcastle	30	45	46	47
Birmingham	196	217	188	235
Sandwell	19	21	34	38
Ealing London Borough Council	32	43	76	76
Havering LBC	14	18	23	25
Tower Hamlets LBC	12	27	28	35
Westminster LBC	140	111	144	201

What this random selection of local authority returns demonstrates is that, starting from a very low base at the point when homelessness figures overall were at an all-time peak, those found to be homeless and vulnerable due to old age by homelessness officers all over England, have increased in number steadily and unspectacularly ever since. The trend is similar in all geographic areas, in London and other big cities, county towns and small district councils.

It also became clear, in the course of this research, that these figures are understated for reasons which relate to local practice and interpretation by officers.

For example, the Code of Guidance requires that, in addition to considering cases in which a person may be over 60 and vulnerable, an authority must also evaluate vulnerability in cases of 'mental illness' or 'physical handicap'. The quarterly returns provided to the DoE also make this distinction of category.

Discussions with officers at local authority level reveal that some of the people in the latter two categories may also be elderly; practice varies as to the statistical category in which they are recorded. Nearly 10% of authorities surveyed said that some proportion of cases involving elderly people would be recorded in these other categories.

In discussion with groups of practitioners a number of common themes emerged:

officers frequently make conscious efforts to avoid facing older people with the complex processes involved in being assessed as homeless, vulnerable and in need.

This results, 'more often than not' in cases not being recorded in official figures. On the other hand, 80% of councils surveyed also said that they would accept elderly applicants in many cases who were not without a home or imminently so, if their current property was unsuitable. For some authorities it is more convenient or quicker to treat such people as homeless rather than to offer a transfer through normal council procedures. One authority said that 50% of its older cases fell into this category.

Discussion with housing association officers, especially in London and the home counties, also reveals that significant numbers of older people who are about to lose their home apply, and are accepted, for associations' sheltered accommodation without seeking help from the council homelessness unit and are therefore not recorded as homeless.

This phenomenon was particularly prevalent in areas where associations had surplus or void sheltered stock to fill, and where a threat of homelessness was related to failure to maintain mortgage payments.

The Code of Guidance makes clear that there are no simple tests of reasonableness in this situation and there is no doubt that a wide range of practice and interpretation operates in the field, much of it leading to an understatement of the true position.

Some comparisons with Wales and Scotland

While this research has concentrated on the position in English authorities. it has been possible to look briefly at the Welsh and Scottish position, utilising Welsh Office figures and some recent research among Scottish councils.

Wales

Statistics for Wales indicate a very similar trend to that in England, in which the total of families accepted as in priority need has been falling consistently since 1992, the proportion of those vulnerable by reason of old age is increasing. Table 3 suggests the same scale of small but inexorable increase.

Scotland

Recent research into the phenomenon of homelessness among older people in Scotland by Wilson (1995) makes a series of recommendations essentially related to the Scottish context of housing policy, but at the same time provides some interesting parallels with the situation in England.

The way in which Scottish Office statistics are analysed, Wilson argues, makes it difficult, if not impossible to get an accurate picture of trends.

The only figures for older people refer to 'single elders: retirement age and above' which are set out in Table 4 of the Scottish Office Statistical bulletin (HAG 1994/93). This therefore omits couples entirely. Wilson is able to demonstrate, from council records, that between 9% and 34% of older people presenting as homeless were, in fact, couples.

Moreover, the Scottish Office's own central research unit has demonstrated that older people represent about 7% of councils' total homeless applicants (Evans et al, 1994).

Similar issues of interpretation at local authority level and the treatment of age 60 or 65 as the official definition of 'old' occur in Scotland as in England, which further blurs the position, but Wilson believes, at a conservative estimate, that between 1,400 and 1,500 older households annually become homeless and are dealt with by local authorities. He does not report the official figures but suggests that they are substantially less than his research reveals.

Who is old?

Survey data for this project suggests that over 70% of councils interpret the DoE Code of Guidance as requiring them to treat all over-60s applicants as elderly and therefore as vulnerable by reason of age. This was true throughout the South and South East although many Northern authorities differentiate between males and females, using 65 as the trigger date for men. A minority tended to consider the actual circumstances involved and therefore to accept some applicants of 58, and others not until they were in their 70s.

Table 3: Homeless households accepted for rehousing by local authorities, Wales (1992-95)

	1992	1993	1994	1995
Total accepted in priority need	7,332	7,757	6,874	5,923
Vulnerable through old age	359	335	348	308
% of total	4.89	4.31	5.0	5.2

Note: The figures are derived from 37 Welsh councils prior to local government review in 1996.

It is also clear from the data that all authorities attempt to avoid responding to older homeless applicants by offering temporary accommodation or Bed & Breakfast hotels. Permanent secure tenancies or nomination to a housing association tenancy are invariably the first response unless the circumstances are of an emergency nature.

What constitutes homelessness?

A large majority of the authorities surveyed reported that applicants in the 'old age' category would be considered if they were in unsuitable accommodation, even if they had not lost or were about to lose their home. In many cases the home had only become unsuitable as impairment, frailty, disability or other factors emerged slowly over time.

When asked why such cases were not dealt with through waiting list and pointing procedures, many said that it was easier and quicker to use the homeless procedures, especially where such cases assist in reducing the void-rates recorded by the authority. Although this distorts recorded statistics somewhat, authorities estimated that such cases amounted at most, to 10% of their annual figure for older applicants.

The role of surplus sheltered housing

Research by Tinker, Wright and Zeilig (1996) has established that 92% of councils and 79% of housing associations have difficult-to-let sheltered housing within their stocks, and the discussions with focus groups of practitioners reinforces this conclusion. But more than that, it suggests that even some newly built specialist dwellings and 'frail elderly' schemes being produced by housing associations are proving exceptionally difficult to attract tenants.

Contrary to Tinker's conclusions, housing professionals in the focus groups argued that this is not simply to do with location or quality, or even size of unit. They feel the same phenomenon appeared to be present in all regions of the country and in rural, urban and metropolitan environments; council officers' responses to the postal survey suggest there are problems in letting newly built, older and traditionally 'popular' stock.

This 'happy coincidence' of surplus sheltered stock, emerging in the 1990s, at the same time as an apparent rise in the numbers of homeless older people leads inevitably to most authorities offering sheltered homes to homeless people whom they categorise as 'old' and vulnerable by reason of age. Indeed, it led one senior officer to say that although there is a growth in the numbers of older people presenting as homeless, "there is no consequent housing problem".

From survey returns from this project, of the responding authorities surveyed, the vast majority utilised sheltered housing as an important resource in meeting the needs of older applicants.

Twenty-three authorities said they frequently used vacant sheltered stock to rehouse older homeless applicants; three said they always do and eight said they occasionally do. Only five councils said they never do.

The increasing evidence of a substantial pool of sheltered stock, of various age, form and location, suggests that it would be appropriate to re-evaluate on a comprehensive basis, the earlier approach and purpose of this kind of housing. It would be important to include even the most modern forms of very sheltered stock in any such review.

Some councils have sought to adapt and up-grade earlier models of sheltered schemes and one major housing association which specialises in this field, and who found that up to 11,000 of its bedsits were, in effect, redundant, have taken a lead within the association sector. Others are providing a wider range of care services and linking them to the demands of care-in-the-community policy initiative, offering a joint approach with social services staff to assessment and allocations in meeting the needs of older clients.

Tinker's study for the DoE (Tinker, Wright and Zeilig, 1996) and her earlier work on very sheltered housing (Tinker, 1989) stress the sensitivities which need to be recognised in any attempt to re-adapt this stock for new uses. Mixing younger with older tenants or those with heavy support needs and those still reasonably able can cause severe management problems.

The careful management of large-scale refurbishment or up-grading in which tenants are required to move out temporarily is essential and implies expert approaches to consultation and communication if upset and confusion are to be avoided.

Successful solutions to these issues are likely to be small in scale, accurately targeted in regard to the kinds of support offered and sharply differentiated in terms of the kinds of needs addressed.

Inevitably the role of wardens in sheltered housing will change too, with the need for retraining and new relationships which identify both housing management roles and those associated with care management.

As Tinker points out, despite exhortations from government that approaches to the reprovisioning of services must be localised and involve close interorganisational working between the key agencies, the "seamless service" referred to in DoE/DoH Circulars is stubbornly slow to emerge.

So that, while it may be coincidentally convenient that surpluses of this stock are available at a time of greater homelessness among older people – and are convenient as a solution – it is in policy terms important to consider the possibilities of a more structured and coherent strategy which seeks, on the one hand, to quantify the needs arising for supported housing, demands for adaptations, for more intensive care and for a 'lifetime homes' approach to accommodating those with support needs, and on the other the possibilities for redesign, adaptation and imaginative re-use of such stock.

These questions are not the prime concern of this paper, but do suggest the need to do further research, in the context of the inter-face between social services and housing agencies, followed by some authoritative guidance to social landlords of all kinds.

Respondents also indicated that where sheltered housing was not available ground floor or bungalow units are offered in many cases. Since all authorities operate a 'one offer only' policy to homeless applicants, there are no records of refusals in any category of offer, even where apparently difficult-to-let studio flats are utilised.

It is pertinent to point out that all the authorities indicating that they never offer sheltered housing to older homeless applicants were situated in the North, North-West and North-East regions, re-flecting the lower percentages of sheltered housing in all categories, in those regions (McCafferty, 1995).

5
Major causes of loss of home

Table 4: Main causes of home loss (1992-95)

	%		%
Partnership breakdown	39	Landlord action	7
Family dispute	25.5	Emergency (fire etc)	2
Private mortgage failure	15	Street homeless	1
Mortgage failure (Right to Buy)	10	Other	0.5

The survey of local authorities revealed eight specified causes given for older people losing their home (see Table 4).

This reveals two prime groups of linked causes through which older people lose their home; the most prevalent is to do with various kinds of relationship breakdown either within families or of partners. Nearly 65% of cases were related in some way to this phenomenon.

The second most common cause (32%) was reported as being related to financial problems ranging from rent arrears to mortgage failure, or collapse of some inter-familial financial agreement. This Table also establishes how infrequently the street homeless come through the local authority system, with only 1% of street homelessness recorded.

Marriage breakdown and intergenerational conflict

A remarkable outcome of the discussions with practitioners was the scale and complexity of breakdown in interpersonal relations through which older people become homeless.

The scale of conflict – and even violence – within older marriage and the breakdown of relations between the generations within a family raise important questions for late-20th century understanding of family dynamics.

If marriage break-up, so long thought to be a phenomenon of younger partners and transient alliances, is rife among the over 60s, is there perhaps a need, as Johnson (1995) argues, to "recognise that significant changes in family formations and in the life expectation of all who survive into mid-life, represent two of the most fundamental changes in social structure."

This study would support such a view since homelessness can be seen as an extreme outcome of family conflict. In short, to paraphrase Johnson (1995), old age and the family encompass the centre ground of a major policy and political discourse, in which the forces which conspire to render one homeless in later life are as important to understand as they are to combat.

From the case histories below, and observations of council staff, it emerges that retirement from active employment is a time of particular strain in long-standing marriages. Husbands or partners, so long absorbed in work and away from home for most hours of the day, are quite suddenly a permanent and largely unoccupied resident. "Under my feet all day..." was a much used phrase by women interviewed for this project, whose daily life and routine had been thrown into disarray by a partner recently retired, especially where the employment had been demanding and all-absorbing; the ability of partners to realign or renew an earlier joint way of life may be impaired in later life.

Another explanation for partnership breakdown offered by many practitioners was that older people in unsatisfactory relationships who might otherwise put up with less than a perfect marriage, can be influenced by the greater readiness of their married children to sever and start again. "When I saw how much better [my daughter] was after the divorce, I thought, why not me…" was the reported comment of one such applicant.

Many homelessness officers commented upon what was termed 'Autumn relationships' in which people in late middle age who had been widowed or divorced after many years, marry again, perhaps relinquishing a tenancy to move into the new partner's house, only to find that they are incompatible and split up. The case histories demonstrate the many variations on these themes.

Recent research has established that a wide range of factors are involved in the creation of tensions between the generations of families (Clarke et al, 1993). The notion that portrays the family as a place of either peace, harmony and refuge, or as a place of abuse, anger and violence, fails to understand the subtleties and changes over time, of kinship, loyalty and friction which most extended families experience (Bengtson et al, 1996). As these researchers comment, "families are typically the source of our greatest pleasure and our greatest pain through life."

Finance and friction

Sociologists working in this field identify causes of quarrels in families such as child-rearing, ideology, work habits and household management, but in the context of the present research it is the economic and money issues which seem to be at the heart of those conflicts which, in the extreme, result in older people becoming homeless.

During the 1980s many middle-aged people were encouraged to take up the Right to Buy their council home (RTB), with inducements rising to as much as 70% discount. In an environment of rising property values, the possibility of acquiring a capital asset which could be passed on to the next generation was tempting to many thousands of people on low incomes and nearing retirement who would otherwise have been content to remain in the public sector for the rest of their lives.

The idea that the asset could be passed on was equally attractive to both the purchasers and their offspring, many of whom encouraged and contributed to RTB acquisitions (Forrest and Murie, 1990).

However, the evidence of this project (see Table 4) suggests that the dream of home ownership has gone sour for many. The long depression in housing markets, the approach of early retirement, sometimes enforced, and reduced income for large sections of the labour market, has exposed the fragility of the economic judgements made by thousands who were enticed into house purchase, and the insubstantial nature of subsidised markets such as RTB. The response to the postal survey of authorities confirms that in areas where the levels of RTB were high there is a consequential high incidence of homelessness caused by the ultimate failure of such transactions among older purchasers.

A number of examples of intergenerational pacts based upon unsecured financial arrangements, followed by subsequent breakdown due to failure in health or need for care, unforeseen monetary problems or simply disputes and quarrels, have emerged in this research (see case histories). Failing health of a family elder who has perhaps spent much of an active middle life living with married children and assisting with rearing a third generation, leads, in significant numbers of cases, to a disinclination on the part of the householders, to continue the live-in arrangements, sometimes after a spell in hospital, although homelessness officers report strong suspicions of collusion in many such applications.

Violence: a multi-faceted phenomenon

In discussions with focus group meetings of practitioners in widely diverse areas, officers were in agreement that violence, in many forms, formed the basis of an increasing number of cases of homelessness in later years. Case histories, such as those illustrated, told of women being violent to older husbands, of men beating women and of elderly couples being hit and abused by the children with whom they lived.

While elder abuse is a phenomenon well researched in sociological literature (McCreadie, 1996), it is more than a little alarming to find so consistent a thread of violence in all areas and perpetrated by all generations, so extreme as to lead to the loss of home. This indicates that the problem is by no means limited to relations between carers and those they care for, the main concern of modern research (Penhale and Kingston, 1995; Phillipson and Biggs, 1992). Cases related during this project refer not only to physical abuse but to the application of psychological and material pressures and while Penhale and Kingston (1995) refer to the 'appalling' record in the UK in institutional settings, one is led to feel that it is not only a problem for community care or for the poor and those on the fringes of society; it is a housing problem too.

Telling it like it is: some case histories of older homeless people

In order to illustrate the human reality of homelessness and the factors which cause it, the remainder of this chapter is devoted to the stories of people with first-hand experience of losing their home.

What follows is a series of mini case histories, some told by the people interviewed for this research and others related by the case officers who assessed the applicants under the homelessness procedures. Some are edited versions of case notes.

They present a graphic illustration of the complex vagaries of life for people in middle and old age and the factors which lead them to have no secure and safe place to call home. What is encouraging is the way in which the 'system' is able to respond, at the point of crisis, and to offer safe and speedy solutions.

This is certainly true of those coming through the local authority housing department route, when the loss of home is the only or dominant issue. For those whom we have described as having more complex, long-term problems, illness or personality conflicts, satisfactory outcomes are slower to emerge and are more prone to break down.

Taken as a whole these cases present a quite varied picture of what is meant by homelessness as it is experienced by those who meet this most fundamental form of ontological insecurity, and the way in which, in late 20th century Britain, the community responds to their need.

Case studies

Family promises that come to nothing

John and **Irene** had been council tenants for many years and had brought up a family of four. They had never thought of going into home ownership because John was an unskilled, low wage earner and they had been happy as tenants of a 'good' council. In 1987, their elder son married and, in a good job, suggested they should buy their four-bedroomed, semi-detached home because they would get it with a 60% discount, in a rising market and would have a major asset to pass on to their children. He offered to provide the deposit for a loan and would pay the bulk of the monthly instalments, on the understanding that the house would be willed to him. The other children had no objections.

By 1995, John and Irene were in their 60s; John had been compulsorily retired and only had a state pension. They were considering moving to smaller accommodation and would have liked to think that a council sheltered scheme could help them when Irene's heart condition got worse. The son's own marriage then failed and with maintenance payments to his wife he said he could no longer afford to pay the mortgage costs he had promised his parents. In due course, after serious family quarrels, the mortgage was foreclosed and the house sold. John and Irene were offered a studio flat in a sheltered scheme, which they find cramped and isolating. John said, however, that he had no choice but to accept.

After the army it was downhill all the way ...

Alec served more than 29 years in the army and although he had been married, he had long ago lost touch with his family. On discharge he worked in security, in hotels and as a hospital porter, and lived in a variety of tied flats, rented bed-sits and in a Salvation Army hostel.

After being sacked from his last job he drifted onto the streets and lived rough in Liverpool, moving to Birmingham and then London. He begged on occasion and used soup kitchens. Aged 56, he then became seriously ill with pneumonia and was taken to hospital, eventually arriving back in Liverpool under social services care, where he now lives in a hostel for older people in need of rehabilitation. He hopes he will not have to leave.

Teenage bully who drove granny to despair

Mrs Smith had lived with her son and daughter-in-law ever since she was widowed 25 years ago. She had her own room and had worked when younger. She had also contributed her share to the household costs and had played a major role in rearing three children of the family. Recently, however, she has become the victim of regular violence by her 15-year-old granddaughter, but does not feel able to tell the parents, partly because of threats of further violence and partly because of the family upset it would cause. She sought advice from CAB and was referred to the council, where she was accepted as both homeless and vulnerable by reason of age (she is 71). She was offered a flat in a category II sheltered scheme of a local housing association.

Mortgage failure and disintegration

Thomas is 62 and was discovered by an environmental health officer sleeping in the stairwell of a council flatblock. His house had been repossessed some months earlier. He had severe drink problems, was unkempt and incontinent, suffering amnesia and confusion as a result of alcohol addiction. He was referred to the homelessness unit who made an immediate referral to the psychiatric unit at the local hospital where he spent 14 months as an inpatient undergoing rehabilitation. When ready for discharge he was referred again to the housing department where he was rehoused directly into an independent flat, supported by a personal care package from social services under the care in the community programme.

She beat him and stabbed him for ten years!

John is 62 and approached the homelessness unit of his London borough claiming serious violence by his partner with whom he had lived as man-and-wife for many years. This was a result of his partner's alcohol problem and had been evident for eight to ten years.

During this time he had suffered a broken leg, a fractured jaw and had been stabbed on more than one occasion. He said that while he was working full-time he could cope but since retirement the problem had worsened. Despite police involvement on many occasions the most recent attack had resulted in hospital care. The house had been bought under RTB about a year ago and both parties' solicitors were discussing a sale. He was assessed as homeless and vulnerable due to age and rehoused immediately.

They bit off more than they could chew!

Mr and Mrs Y are 67 and 62 respectively. They were council tenants of a metropolitan borough in the North West for a number of years. Both worked for the council. They exercised their Right to Buy in 1983 and had a council mortgage for £14,000.

Later the house was remortgaged for £30,000 in order to upgrade, double glaze and replace fitments. But this meant repayments going up to £750 per month and the couple fell into serious arrears, especially after Mr Y retired. They eventually gave up the keys and the house was sold but left a substantial shortfall which they are still paying at £50 per month.

They moved in with a widowed friend but when the friend remarried they were asked to leave and presented to the council as homeless. As Mrs Y now had mobility problems they were offered the tenancy of a ground floor flat by the council from whom they originally bought.

She decided she'd had enough!

Fred was divorced some years ago but continued to live with his ex-wife in her council house. When he was 60 she said she had "had enough" and insisted he leave.

Since the house was an 'out borough' unit he went to the local council who rehoused him into sheltered housing as his name was not on the tenancy agreement.

He worked till he dropped – and then had no home

Patrick came from Ireland in the 1960s and worked on road schemes and building sites all over England. Mostly he lived in caravans and lodgings provided by contractors for whom he worked. He was still doing such work at 68 but became ill and was taken to hospital in June 1996. The hospital would not discharge him until a proper home was found and a niece allowed him to live in her cottage in Norfolk on a temporary basis. He is now 75. The cottage was in such serious disrepair that it was declared unfit by the environmental health officer. Patrick was accepted by the niece's local council as unintentionally homeless and offered category II sheltered housing.

Threatened by his wife and son

Percy was being beaten up and threatened by his son. He is 76 and lived with his wife and son in a council tenancy. His wife had tried before to remove his name from the tenancy without success and an RTB claim had been denied. In 1995 he agreed to relinquish tenancy rights to escape violence and went to live with his brother but in due course that house was destroyed by a fire. He was rehoused by the council in an emergency hostel and transferred to self-contained temporary flat while enquiries continue. An offer of sheltered studio flat is most likely, which Percy says will be very adequate.

The decline and fall of a prosperous professional

John and Jane, both 79, were well-off professional people from Yorkshire. He had been a senior bank manager until retirement and Jane had been active in the church and charity work. On his retirement in 1980 John had a good pension, a comfortable five-bedroomed house in the country with a half acre of garden. He expected to have a comfortable and active retirement. He worried about the up-keep of so large a house but wanted plenty of space for the grandchildren to visit.

Their son, who was married with three children and lived in the west country, was managing director of a prosperous hotel chain and lived in a 'mansion'. The families were close.

In the late 1980s they were encouraged by the son to sell up, to come and live in a self-contained part of the son's house; the son also encouraged his father to invest his surplus capital in the business and to become a non-executive director.

By 1990 the business was contracting and began to lose money. The son remortgaged his home. John gave him unsecured loans but the business was forced into liquidation; the 'mansion' had to be sold. The son then bought a run-down seaside hotel in which to create a new business. He installed his parents in a 'penthouse flat' at the top of the hotel while he ran the rest as a going concern. By this time family relationships had deteriorated; in Jane's words they reached the "rock-bottom of hostility". In 1995 the elderly couple, now 78, were forced to move from the penthouse to a damp and cramped basement of the hotel. All their investment in the business had been lost and the son was unable to repay loans. Their health broke down.

They approached the council in 1996 claiming homelessness on the grounds that it was unreasonable for them to continue living in the basement. They were accepted and rehoused into a frail elderly sheltered scheme and were offered a two-bedded flat on the ground floor.

The ins and outs of hostel life

Jock who is 62, originally came from Glasgow where his ex-wife and children still live. He was in scrap metal, a trade he continued when he came to Wales. He is well known to most of Swansea's homeless charities and aid agencies, having gone from one to another over many years, sometimes sleeping rough for a while.

In 1993 he was referred to a specialist project which offers accommodation to older people with a strong bias toward rehabilitation and support. For a while he was happy, his alcohol consumption was self-controlled and his health improved. He asked to be rehoused in a self-contained flat which was achieved with the help of a housing association.

However, this was not a happy move and drink and self-neglect meant he became a problem tenant. A social worker and community psychiatric nurse who had been supporting him eventually got him back into the hostel where he continued to be a difficult and disruptive influence.

Once again he pressed for an independent flat and, despite advice, was again offered an association flatlet. He refuses help, has poor health and retains only a tenuous grasp on his alcohol consumption. However, those who try to support him say he is quite happy with the lifestyle he has chosen. He does not consider that he has ever been 'homeless'.

Summer at the seaside – and how it turned to winter

Ron: when Ron retired in 1988 he and his wife sold up and bought a mobile home at the seaside. They lived in this in the summer and, when the site closed in October, returned to live with a daughter for the winter. Ron died two years ago. His wife Joyce does not cope well.

This year she failed to pay the site rent and was given notice; her daughter's marriage failed, requiring her to move to a smaller home in which she cannot continue to accommodate her mother.

Joyce's application to the council was accepted, she was assessed as unintentionally homeless and vulnerable due to age. She was offered a non-secure tenancy in a one-bed ground floor flat but refused it because she did not like the location. The council issued a notice under Section 64 and she was offered further advice about private renting possibilities.

Summary

What these case histories demonstrate above all is that once older people engage with 'the system' the outcome in housing terms is usually swift and satisfactory, particularly for those dealt with by local authority home-lessness units. The assessment process itself is, for the most part, sensitive to the conditions of the applicant. However, for those who come via the streets or with a range of other personal problems, it is not so clear that the path to settled and secure accommodation is as smooth, or as permanent. Nor is it clear that clients with support needs are assisted adequately beyond the brief respite offered in winter shelters and crisis projects. In the next chapter we look more closely at this group and the outcomes they experience.

6
The chronically homeless: the missing dimension

As explained at the outset of this project, it became clear at once that to quantify the numbers of older homeless people by reference to statistics from local authorities in the DoE's P1 (E) (Housing) database would result in missing an unknown number of people who do not utilise local authority homelessness systems.

It is clearly beyond the scope of this research to undertake a full-scale survey of the many hundreds of voluntary hostels, group homes and 'rough sleeper' initiatives in which many older homeless people survive, either temporarily or serially.

Rather, the intention here is to give substance to the argument that any quantification of trends in older homelessness must have regard to the numbers not found in official statistics for whom lack of a home is just one among many problems; and secondly, which of them, reasonably, can be termed 'older'.

It will be seen from Crane's review (1994) of earlier research, discussed in Chapter 3 above, that such investigations as have been carried out among hostel dwellers and street homeless people reveal that anything from 18% to 35% of such people are 60+ (Crane, 1994). Typically people in these circumstances are said to exhibit 'lifelong difficulties with other people', or to have suffered trauma such as bereavement or a disruptive childhood. Low skills and poor education are often evident. Frequently they are subject to alcohol or drug dependency and exhibit what Merton (1957) terms 'retreatist' behaviour.

Crane's most recent research in this field strengthens the indications in this and earlier work that among the prime triggers of older street homelessness, mental ill-health, disrupted family life, ejection from the

cocooning effect of institutional life, and bereavement, are constant factors (Crane, 1997).

She reports that over half of those who achieve resettlement become homeless again and, oddly, that some of her sample stayed on the street at night despite having accommodation available.

This suggests strongly that unless a carefully designed degree of support is offered as part of the rehousing package, resettlement is likely not to be a success in the long term; a point which many front-line workers have been making to social workers from the inception of the Care in the Community reforms.

Crane, whose focus was London, Leeds, Sheffield and Manchester, recommends much more work in identifying older people at risk, the employment of specialist out-reach workers to make contact with those who have become isolated and an intensive programme of resettlement, including the provision of long-term support. It is argued in this context that 'direct access' accommodation should only ever be seen as an interim solution.

It is evident then that the housing histories of many people who utilise hostels, sleep rough or exist in a twilight world of institutions, is transient and often unstable. It only rarely results in their utilising the formal processes of assessment under the 1985 Act. For example, this research suggests that only 1% of applicants to housing departments are 'street homeless' (Table 4).

This is not to suggest that the two cohorts of 'official' and 'unofficial' homeless are mutually and rigidly compartmentalised. As the case histories indicate, it is possible that rough sleepers and others can be brought within the formal networks and benefit from supported social housing; equally, those who lose a stable home can, and do, sometimes fall through the net and slide into an existence on the streets or into a transient half-life of flop houses, night shelters or vagrancy.

It is also evident that external factors such as the impact of economic recession on unskilled labour, the restrictive approach to social welfare and the failure of some Care in the Community programmes, results in many of those who rely on institutions or tied housing, losing such security of tenure as these traditionally offered.

Little seems to have changed in the decade and more since those earlier research conclusions. This chapter attempts, by way of a random snapshot, to get some idea of the current scale of the phenomenon and the frequency with which this cohort appears in the wider population of people for whom the lack of a home is only one of a range of problems in coping with day-to-day living. It has been possible to utilise statistics from several voluntary projects and from the research material of national bodies such as 'Crisis' and Shelter.

The specialist hostel populations

In a voluntary project in Cardiff set up in 1992 to attempt the rehabilitation of older people, the 42 residents have been referred by other agencies or come directly from the street or another hostel. 36 of the residents are over 50. In this case rehabilitation means for many a move on to secure tenancies, and the project has now become part of a registered housing association in order to facilitate this process.

In North West London a similar but larger specialist housing association provided, in 1995/96, residential services to over 500 older homeless people over 50; it delivered daycare services to over 800 older homeless people, 30% of whom were women without homes. It also provided specifically targeted

accommodation, support and specialist help to over 1,300 such clients.

In fact, this body manages 1,200 units of accommodation throughout London and the South East and of the 3,511 lettings made in 1995/96, 44% of tenants had slept on the street the previous night and 38% were over 50 years of age.

In one 400-bed London hostel for the homeless, 64% of residents are reported to be over 50.

What these projects seem to confirm is that in any cohort of homeless people, there is indeed a significant number of people over 50 who, in terms of need, ability and state of health, do indeed need to be included in the term 'older'.

Users of crisis shelters

But perhaps the sharpest focus of any snapshot in this field can be obtained by looking at emergency schemes that attract people to emergency schemes, crisis shelters and projects of the kind highlighted at Christmas and through the government's rough sleepers initiative (RSI).

It is in these projects, aimed at all vagrant people, that some judgement can be made about the numbers of older people within the whole group.

Table 5 analyses the age and sex of those who were assisted in winter crisis shelters during the winter of 1994/95, in five central London schemes.

These figures demonstrate the significantly larger male clientele and the consequently larger percentage of older men than women to be found on the streets. It illustrates too, the heavy concentration of older people in the 50/60 age group, tailing off sharply after 60.

Table 6 is derived from counts undertaken by the Homeless Network on 23 May 1996 among those living on the street in the London RSI zones of central and Whitechapel and City (West and Central Zone [WACZO]) areas.

Table 5: Numbers of people using five London Crisis shelters, by age and gender (Winter 1994/95) (%)

	Leighton Road (London Borough of Camden)		Neville House (St Mungo's Association)		Southwark Street (Crisis)		Turnstile House (English Churches Housing)		Victoria House (Salvation Army Housing)	
	F	M	F	M	F	M	F	M	F	M
	91	n/a	55	268	29	45	63	293	n/a	53
Under 18	2		0	0	6	0	1	0.3		0
18-25	29		24	15	24	14	38	24		11
26-35	30		35	28	35	31	18	30		23
36-49	29		30	37	28	31	27	30		40
50-59	9		4	13	7	13	14	10		18
Over 60	1		7	7	0	11	2	6		8
Average age (years)	33		36	40	25	35	33	36		40

Source: 'Crash' (1995)

In undertaking this count, researchers estimated that in the central area the majority had been on the street for more than five years and ten out of seventeen over-60s had done so.

The 'Winterwatch' programme is a series of shelters outside of the zones targeted for the RSI. It is organised by the housing charities 'Crisis' and Shelter. In a snapshot survey of 26 projects nationwide, during the winter of 1995/96, 299 users completed questionnaires (see Table 7). 252 were male and 47 female. 96% described themselves as white, 1% as black and 3% as of mixed race.

Researchers undertaking this work suggest that in the age group 40/59 approximately 33% were over 50 years of age.

These three statistical snapshots at least confirm the volume and consistency with which older people appear in the peripheral and precarious shelters and hostels of our cities. They also confirm the proposition that until they appear in more formal, official databases, they will inevitably form a 'hidden' aspect of the overall picture of homeless older people in Britain.

Table 6: Rough sleepers in London RSI zones, by age (23 May 1996)

	Central		WACZO	
Age range	Number	(%)	Number	%
Under 18	6	(3)	–	–
18-25	53	(23)	3	(9)
26-49	100	(44)	15	(45.5)
50-59	40	(18)	14	(42.5)
Over 60	28	(12)	1	(3)
Total	**227**	**100**	**33**	**100**

Source: Homeless Network

Table 7: Occupants of winter shelters not in RSI zones, by age and location (Winter 1995/96)

Agency location	Under 18	18-25	26-39	40-59	Over 60	Total
Alfreton	2	4				6
Birmingham		1	4	1		6
Bristol		3	17	7		27
Canterbury		4	2			6
Chester			1	4	2	7
Croydon		2	4			6
Dundee		3	6	2	1	12
Edinburgh	1	5	3	10	5	24
Glasgow - Blue Triangle		2	1			3
Glasgow - Wayside Club			3	2		5
Godalming		2	2	1		5
Leamington		1	2			3
Lincoln - Nomad Trust	1	5	2	3		11
Manchester	1	8	8	6	2	25
Newham	1	2	5	6		14
North Herts		1	3	1		5
Norwich		5	9	7		21
Reading		5	7	2	1	15
Southampton		3	5	4		12
Stoke-on-Trent	1	5	2	2		10
Swansea		5	6	5		16
Wallasey		3	9			12
Watford	1	1	3	4		9
Wearside	6	9		6		21
Winchester			3	3		6
Woking	2	2	2			6
Total	**16**	**81**	**109**	**76**	**11**	

Source: Crisis (1996)

7
Conclusions and recommendations

A number of conclusions are suggested by the findings of this research, although there are some ambiguities and even contradictions which emerge from the facts. It is also difficult to establish coherence with regard to the two distinct cohorts which are discussed here.

There is no doubt that between 1992 and 1995 the experience in local government housing departments was of increasing percentages of older clients within the totals of homeless applicants processed, although for most the numerical significance was small. But the over-riding cautionary note, in discussing the issues, is to do with the probability that there are underlying cyclical reasons for the growth which is revealed.

Both economic and demographic cycles may explain the phenomenon. First, the undoubted increase, in the population as a whole, of older people is one which has very wide implications for virtually all aspects of social policy, and may be one reason why larger numbers of older people now emerge within the homelessness figures.

Second, the persistent depression in housing markets, only now coming to an end, has lasted since 1989 and may also explain why so many older people, who purchased when they were still in work and in younger middle age, have been unable to sustain owner-occupation in the period under review.

Nevertheless, with these underlying concerns, it is possible to reach some specific conclusions as set out below:

~ Between 1992 and 1995 homelessness among older people has, at best, not reduced to the same extent as in the case of families with young children, and at worst, it is on the increase, especially if the figures for vagrancy and street homelessness are added to the official statistics.

~ Local authority statistics show that while percentage increases are substantial in many areas, the numerical increase is less significant because of low base figures.

~ However, there may be as much as 10% understatement of the total of older homeless, for the reasons elicited in this research.

~ The evidence of earlier research and current statistics suggests that the numbers of older people on the streets or in marginal or precarious housing conditions remains stubbornly consistent over time and that they are not benefiting from the care in the community reforms to the extent that they might.

~ Because of an apparent increase in vacant sheltered housing among most local authorities and housing associations, the volume of older homeless people identified and assessed by local authorities do not present a major housing problem; the issue is rather one of social concern and appropriate support at the time of crisis.

~ There is no unanimity among local authority homelessness units about what is defined as 'old age', and a variety of practice in regard to responses made to cases accepted for rehousing. This may include some understatement of totals.

~ The majority of local authorities use vacant sheltered housing widely in response to older homeless applicants and none resort to temporary accommodation or Bed & Breakfast as a first response, except in overnight emergencies.

~ There is a strong case for accepting that people of 50 and over, especially when they have multiple personal or health problems underlying their lack of a secure home, should be treated as old in the formal guidance issued by the DoE.

~ The overwhelming causes of loss of home, among those assessed by local authorities as homeless and vulnerable by reason of age, relate to family disputes and partnership breakdown in later life; a secondary cause is financial failure to sustain either rental or mortgage costs.

~ Many people who were motivated to purchase a public sector property in the 1980s have subsequently failed to maintain owner-occupied status. There is evidence that in some cases the original purchase was financed by other family members under informal arrangements subsequently not sustained.

~ The alleged degree of domestic violence against older people of both sexes, and leading to homelessness is significant and worrying.

It is possible then, from the factors revealed in this research, to suggest recommendations for practitioners and policy makers in the DoE, local authorities and other social landlord bodies which address the above conclusions in a positive and practical way.

Recommendations

~ Further guidance should be issued for the benefit of local authorities in the completion of DoE returns (PI(E)(Housing) to ensure consistency in (a) the categorisation of cases accepted as homeless and in priority need, and (b) the definition of 'old age'.

~ The government should institute a system for the comprehensive recording, monitoring and differentiating of numbers of older people who are among the street homeless and those utilising night shelters, temporary hostels and schemes such as 'Crisis at Christmas'. In this context, people of 50 and over should come within the definition of old age.

This recommendation should be construed in the context of monitoring the government's RSI.

~ Local authorities should be empowered to offer a range of mortgage support mechanisms to assist older RTB purchasers to maintain their tenure through periods of financial crisis.

~ The priority given by social services departments in the provision of personal care packages to older people who need both accommodation and support, should be enhanced. The link between temporary accommodation, shelters and direct access hostels, and those responsible for the strategic planning of community care, should be given greater emphasis.

~ There should be further research, particularly in relation to the re-use of surplus sheltered housing stocks of registered social landlords, with a view to ensuring that it makes a larger contribution to the combined care, support and accommodation needs of people assisted within the community care initiative. Attention should be paid to examples of good practice in this respect.

References

Anderson, I. et al (1993) *Single homeless people*, London: HMSO.

Arblaster, L., Conway, J., Foreman, A. and Hawtin, M. (1996) *Asking the impossible? A study of inter-agency working to address the housing, health and social care needs of people in general needs housing*, Bristol: The Policy Press.

Audit Commission (1989) *Housing the homeless: the local authority role*, London: HMSO.

Bassuck, E.L. and Buckner, C. (1992) 'Out of mind, out of sight', *American Journal of Orthopsychiatry*, vol 62, no 3, pp 330-31.

Bengtson, V., Biblarz, T., Clarke, E., Giarrusso, R., Roberts, R., Kichlin-Klonsky, J. and Silverstein, M. (1996) 'Intergenerational relationships and ageing', Paper presented to the Annual Conference of the British Society of Gerontology.

Clarke, E., Preston, M., Raskin, J. and Bengston, V. (1993) 'Family conflict in older parent–adult child relationships', Paper read to the AGM of Gerontological Society of America, New Orleans, November.

Cohen, C.I. and Sokolovsky, J. (1989) *Old men of the bowery: strategies for survival among the homeless*, New York: The Guildford Press.

Crane, M. (1993) *Elderly homeless people sleeping on the streets of inner London: an exploratory study*, London: Age Concern Institute of Gerontology.

Crane, M. (1994) 'Elderly homeless people: elusive subjects and slippery concepts', *Ageing and Society*, vol 14, Part 4, December.

Crane, M. (1997) *Homeless truths: challenging the myths about older homeless people*, London: Help the Aged/Crisis.

Douglass, R. et al (1988) *Aged, adrift and alone: Detroit's elderly homeless*, Ypsilanti: Eastern Michigan University Press.

Evans, R. (1994) *The Code of Guidance on homelessness in Scotland*, Edinburgh: Scottish Office.

Forrest, R. and Murie, A. (1990) *Selling the welfare state*, London: Routledge.

Johnson, M.I. (1995) 'Interdependency and the generational compact', *Ageing and Society*, vol 15, pp 243-65.

Lodge Patch, I. (1971) 'Homeless men in London: demographic findings in a lodging house sample', *British Journal of Psychiatry*, vol 118, pp 313-17.

London Research Centre (LRC) (1996) *Trends in homelessness in London in the 1990s*, London: LRC.

McCafferty, P. (1995) *Living independently*, London: HMSO.

McCreadie, C. (1991) *Elder abuse: an exploratory study*, London: Age Concern Institute of Gerontology.

Merton, R. (1957) *Social theory and social structure*, Glencoe; Illinois Free Press.

Penhale, B. and Kingston, P. (1995) 'Elder abuse: an overview', *Health & Social Care in the Community*, vol 3, pp 311-20.

Phillipson, C. and Biggs, S. (1992) *Understanding elder abuse*, London: Longman.

Rich, D., Rich, T. and Mullins, L. (eds) (1995) *Old and homeless – double jeopardy: an overview of current practice and policies*, Westport: Auburn House.

Rossi, P. (1989) *Down and out in America*, Chicago: University of Chicago Press.

Sheppard, H.L. (1995) Foreword, in D. Rich, T. Rich and L. Mullins, *Old and homeless – double jeopardy*, Westport: Auburn House.

Tinker, A. (1989) *An evaluation of very sheltered housing*, London: HMSO.

Tinker, A., Wright, F. and Zeilig, H. (1996) *Difficult-to-let sheltered housing*, London: Age Concern Institute of Gerontology/ HMSO.

Wilson, D. (1995) *We will need to take you in ...*, Edinburgh: The Scottish Council for Single Homeless.

Appendix

Incidence of acceptance of homelessness cases of people in priority need 'by reason of old age' (1992-95)

Authority	1992	1993	1994	1995
North Somerset	12	19	20	21
East Cambridgeshire	2	7	9	11
Peterborough	7	6	16	16
Halton	16	17	18	20
Carrick	14	16	18	29
Bath	10	13	17	17
Harlow	6	15	19	17
Plymouth	54	54	60	61
Hove	17	14	29	37
Maldon	7	10	12	14
Tewkesbury	2	8	6	9
Great Grimsby	5	11	14	15
Maidstone	7	8	10	18
Tonbridge Wells	12	20	16	27
Blackpool	3	8	8	9
Pendle	5	6	20	17
Ribble Valley	2	4	6	7
Leicester	47	51	48	64
Northern Kesteven	5	4	6	9
Broadland	14	16	11	21
Blyth Valley	10	11	14	16
Bridgnorth	5	6	7	9
South Somerset	13	23	25	33
Lichfield	8	8	11	12
St Edmundsbury	5	6	6	7
Arun	11	24	25	31
Crawley	10	15	17	18
Horsham	3	6	10	10
Worthing	7	10	13	14
Thamesdown	15	21	26	33
Trafford	50	56	77	66
Liverpool	37	38	47	43
Sefton	21	28	31	34
Newcastle	30	45	46	47
Sunderland	14	11	15	24
Birmingham	196	217	188	235
Coventry	11	5	9	12
Dudley	32	28	44	43
Sandwell	19	21	34	38
Calderdale	19	21	30	37
Ealing	32	43	76	76
Harrow	32	39	44	53
Havering	14	18	23	25
Lewisham	17	22	30	53
Tower Hamlets	12	27	28	35
Westminster	140	111	144	201